WOLFGANG AMADEUS MOZART

COMPLETE
SERENADES
in Full Score

SERIES 1

From the
Breitkopf & Härtel Complete Works Edition

DOVER PUBLICATIONS, INC.
New York

Published in Canada by General Publishing Company, Ltd., 30 Lesmill Road, Don Mills, Toronto, Ontario.

Published in the United Kingdom by Constable and Company, Ltd., 3 The Lanchesters, 162–164 Fulham Palace Road, London W6 9ER.

This Dover edition, first published in 1990, is a republication of portions of Serie 9 and 10 from *Wolfgang Amadeus Mozart's Werke. Kritisch durchgesehene Gesammtausgabe,* originally published by Breitkopf & Härtel, Leipzig, in 1880 and 1881. Lists of instruments have been added.

Manufactured in the United States of America

Dover Publications, Inc., 31 East 2nd Street, Mineola, N.Y. 11501

Library of Congress Cataloging-in-Publication Data

Mozart, Wolfgang Amadeus, 1756–1791.
  Complete serenades.
  Reprint. Originally published: Leipzig: Breitkopf & Härtel, 1880–1883 (from Serie 9, 10, and 13 of Wolfgang Amadeus Mozart's Werke. Kritisch durchgesehene Gesammtausgabe).
  Contents: Series 1. Serenade in D major for strings and winds, K. 185/167a (1773). Serenade in D major for strings and winds, K. 204/213a (1775). Serenata notturna : for strings and timpani, K. 239 (1776). Serenade in D major for strings and winds, K. 250/248b (1776) : Haffner. Serenade in C minor for 8 winds, K. 388/384a (1782 or 1783). A musical joke = Ein musikalischer Spass : for strings and horns, K. 522 (1787)—Series 2. Serenade in D major for strings and winds, K. 203/189b (1774). Notturno in D major : for four orchestras (strings and horns), K. 286/269a (1776–77). Serenade in D major for strings, winds, and timpani, K. 320 (1779) : Posthorn. Serenade in B-flat major for 13 winds, K. 361/370a (1781 or 1781–4). Serenade in E-flat major for 8 winds, K. 375 (1781). Eine kleine Nachtmusik = A little notturno : for strings, K. 525 (1787).
  1. Suites—Scores. I. Title.
M3.1M9S5 1990   90-751180
ISBN 0-486-26565-X (series 1)
ISBN 0-486-26566-8 (series 2)

CONTENTS

INSTRUMENTATION

Serenade in D Major, K. 185/167a

2 Flutes [Flauti]
2 Oboes [Oboi]
2 Horns (D,F,A) [Corni]
2 Trumpets (D) [Trombe lunghe, Trombe]
Violin solo [Violino Principale, Violino Solo]
Violins I, II [Violino]
Violas
Cellos ⎱ [Basso]
Basses ⎰

Serenade in D Major, K. 204/213a

2 Flutes [Flauti]
2 Oboes [Oboi]
Bassoon [Fagotto]
2 Horns (D,A,G) [Corni]
2 Trumpets (D) [Trombe]
Violin solo [Violino Principale]
Violins I, II [Violino]
Violas
Cellos ⎱ [Basso]
Basses ⎰

Serenata Notturna, K. 239

Orchestra I:
   2 Violins solo [Violino Principale]
   Viola
   Bass
Orchestra II:
   Timpani
   Violins I, II [Violino]
   Violas
   Cellos

"Haffner" Serenade, K. 250/248b

2 Flutes [Flauti]
2 Oboes [Oboi]
2 Bassoons [Fagotti]
2 Horns (D,G,A) [Corni]
2 Trumpets (D) [Trombe]
Violin solo [Violino Principale]
Violins I, II [Violino]
Violas I, II
Cellos ⎱ [Basso]
Basses ⎰

Serenade in C Minor, K. 388/384a

2 Oboes [Oboi]
2 Clarinets (B♭) [Clarinetto]
2 Bassoons [Fagotto]
2 Horns (E♭) [Corni in Es]

A Musical Joke, K. 522

2 Horns (F) [Corni]
2 Violins [Violino]
Viola
Cello ⎱ [Basso]
Bass ⎰

Serenade in D Major
for strings and winds
K. 185/167a

I

Serenade in D Major, K. 185/167a   3

4   Serenade in D Major, K. 185/167a

Serenade in D Major, K. 185/167a

Serenade in D Major, K. 185/167a   19

Menuetto da capo.

Andante grazioso.

Flauti.

Corni in A.

Violino I.

Violino II.

Viola.

Basso.

CODA.

MENUETTO.

TRIO I.

Violino solo.

Violino I.

Violino II.

Viola.

Menuetto da capo.

Serenade in D Major, K. 185/167a

Allegro assai.

·CODA.

Serenade in D Major

for strings and winds

K. 204/213a

44   Serenade in D Major, K. 204/213a

Menuetto.

Oboi.

Corni in D.

Trombe in D.

Violino I.

Violino II.

Viola.

Basso.

f. Menuetto da capo

(Andante.)

Flauto.

Oboe.

Fagotto.

Corno I in D.

Corno II in G.

Violino I.

Violino II.

Viola.

Basso.

(Andante.)

Coda.

Serenade in D Major, K. 204/213a   71

Andantino.

Andantino.

Allegro.

Allegro.

Allegro.

Allegro.

Serenata Notturna

for strings and timpani

K. 239

Menuetto.

Menuetto da capo.

Serenade in D Major ("Haffner")

for strings and winds

K. 250/248b

Allegro molto.

Allegro molto.

"Haffner" Serenade, K. 250/248b

"Haffner" Serenade, K. 250/248b

Menuetto.

Flauti.

Fagotti.

Corni in G.

Violino principale.

Violino I.

Violino II.

Viola I.II.

Basso.

Trio.

"Haffner" Serenade, K. 250/248b

Menuetto da capo.

Rondo.

"Haffner" Serenade, K. 250/248b

138   "Haffner" Serenade, K. 250/248b

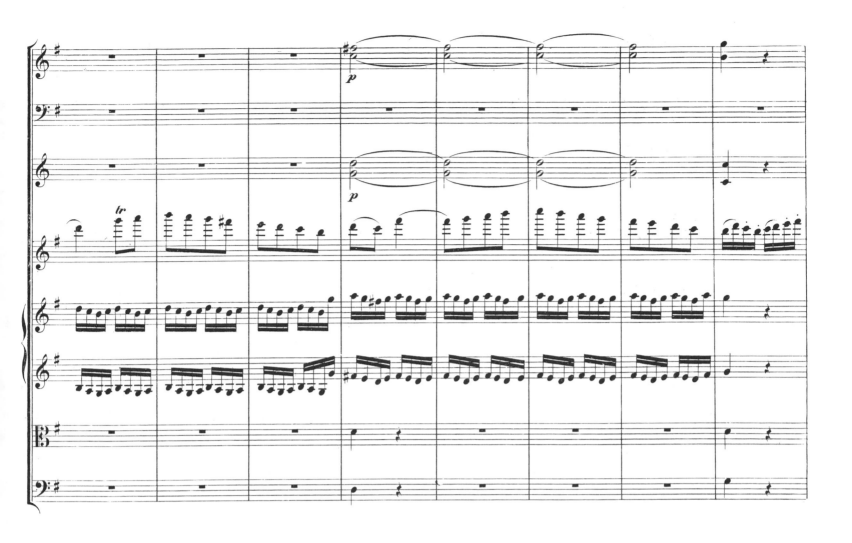

"Haffner" Serenade, K. 250/248b

Menuetto galante.

Oboi.

Fagotti.

Corni in D.

Trombe in D.

Violino I.

Violino II.

Viola I. II.

Basso.

"Haffner" Serenade, K. 250/248b

Trio I.

Menuetto da capo.

"Haffner" Serenade, K. 250/248b   177

Trio II.

Menuetto da capo.

"Haffner" Serenade, K. 250/248b   179

"Haffner" Serenade, K. 250/248b

Serenade in C Minor

for 8 winds

K. 388/384a

Serenade in C Minor, K. 388/384a   205

Trio in Canone al rovescio.

Menuetto da capo.

Allegro.

Allegro.

Serenade in C Minor, K. 388/384a

A Musical Joke
[Ein musikalischer Spass]

for strings and horns

K. 522

MENUETTO.
Maestoso.

Dal segno

A Musical Joke, K. 522